THE CIRCULATORY SYSTEM

A FIRST BOOK

THE CIRCULATORY SYSTEM

FROM HARVEY TO
THE ARTIFICIAL HEART

BY TOM McGOWEN

FRANKLIN WATTS
NEW YORK • LONDON • TORONTO
SYDNEY • 1988

Illustrations by Anne Canevari Green

Photographs courtesy of:
New York Public Library Picture Collection:
pp. 16, 35, 37, 49, 50, 56 (bottom);
The Bettmann Archive, Inc.: pp. 18, 20, 27,
40, 52, 59; Photo Researchers, Inc.:
pp. 45 (Mary Evans Picture Library),
56 (top: Cecil Fox/Science Source),
66 (bottom: Hank Morgan); UPI/Bettmann
Newsphotos: pp. 63, 66 (top).

Library of Congress Cataloging-in-Publication Data

McGowen, Tom.
The circulatory system: from Harvey to the artificial heart / by
Tom McGowen.
p.   cm.—(A First book)
Bibliography: p.
Includes index.
Summary: Describes early theories on how the circulatory system
functions, Harvey's "discovery" of the circulatory system, and
advances since his time in this area of medicine.
ISBN 0-531-10574-1
1. Blood—Circulation—Juvenile literature. 2. Blood—
Circulation—Research—History—Juvenile literature.
3. Cardiovascular system—Physiology—Juvenile literature.
4. Cardiovascular system—Physiology—Research—History—Juvenile
literature. [1. Blood—Circulation. 2. Circulatory system.
3. Heart. 4. Harvey, William, 1578-1657.] I. Title.
QP103.M34   1988   88-231
612'.1—dc19   CIP   AC

FOR
DANNY

CONTENTS

THE CIRCULATORY SYSTEM

CHAPTER

I

EARLY IDEAS

Day and night, day in and day out, whether you are standing, sitting, walking, running, awake, or sleeping, a pair of pumps inside your body works steadily away, pumping fluid through miles of tiny tubes, sending it to all parts of your body, and bringing it back again. The working of those pumps is, quite literally, what keeps you alive.

The pair of pumps is, of course, the organ called the *heart.* The heart is a hollow muscle about the size of a person's fist, divided lengthwise into two parts by a wall of muscle called the *septum.* Each of the parts is divided into two chambers, one above the other, with openings between them.

Through four tubes called *veins*, blood flows from the lungs into the upper chamber on the left side of the heart. The blood contains quantities of the gas called *oxygen*, which is in the air and which is inhaled into the lungs each time a breath is taken. The lower chamber steadily squeezes and relaxes, squeezes and relaxes, and each time it relaxes, blood filled with oxygen flows down into it through the opening from the upper chamber. Each time it squeezes, this oxygen-filled blood is squirted into a large tube called the *aorta*, which leads out of the lower chamber and branches out into thousands of smaller tubes called *arteries*,

THE HUMAN HEART

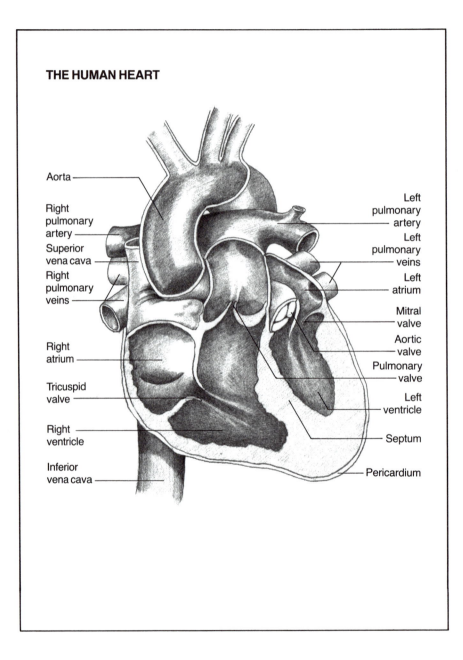

Aorta

Right
pulmonary
artery

Superior
vena cava

Right
pulmonary
veins

Right
atrium

Tricuspid
valve

Right
ventricle

Inferior
vena cava

Left
pulmonary
artery

Left
pulmonary
veins

Left
atrium

Mitral
valve

Aortic
valve

Pulmonary
valve

Left
ventricle

Septum

Pericardium

which reach to all parts of the body. The steady pumping of blood out of the lower chamber on the heart's left side keeps blood moving through all these arteries.

Blood flows through the arteries into tiny tubes called *capillaries*, which pass near every cell in the body. The blood releases the oxygen it is carrying, and the cells use it for fuel, burning it for energy to stay alive. As blood passes by a cell it picks up the waste from previously burned oxygen—in the form of a gas called *carbon dioxide*—and moves out of the capillaries into the veins. Carrying carbon dioxide along with it, it moves through the veins back toward the heart, pushed along by the pressure of the blood behind it. It enters the right side of the heart through two large veins and flows through the top chamber and down into the bottom one.

Like the lower chamber on the left, the lower chamber on the right is also a pump that squeezes and relaxes as the left-hand

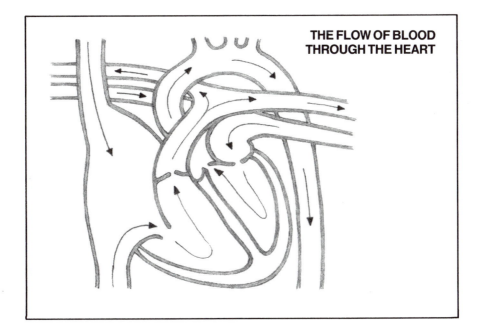

THE FLOW OF BLOOD THROUGH THE HEART

chamber does, only with less strength. It only has to push the carbon-dioxide-carrying blood into the lungs, where the carbon dioxide is released and then forced out of the body when the lungs exhale, or blow out, air. The blood takes on a new supply of oxygen and moves on into the left side of the heart, to begin another journey through the body.

Thus, because the heart is constantly pumping the blood through the body and back to itself in a circular pattern, we call this operation the *circulatory system.* It is the basis of life. If the heart stops and the blood ceases to circulate, or if an injury causes the blood to flow out of the body through an opened artery or vein, so that no blood reaches the cells, the body will die.

Because we understand how the circulatory system works, doctors and other people in the medical profession are able to save millions of lives. We have had this knowledge for only a few hundred years, but it took thousands of years for us to gain.

Even in prehistoric times some men and women were interested in trying to cure sickness and heal injuries, and they studied the bodies of people and animals to find out how the inner parts worked. They realized that the heart and blood were tremendously important, but they did not understand how these things functioned. They could feel and see that human and animal hearts "beat"—but they did not know why. They could see that a body seemed to be filled with blood, but they could not tell where the blood came from and what it was for. Even if you are able to look inside one, you really cannot tell much about what is going on inside a human body, and so ancient people got some odd ideas.

The ancient Egyptians learned a lot about the human body because of the way they embalmed dead people to make them into mummies. In order to mummify a body, embalmers had to cut it open, take out all the organs (heart, lungs, liver, and so on), and then fill the body with sand and chemical salts. Naturally, this gave them the chance to see how the organs were arranged in

THE CIRCULATORY SYSTEM

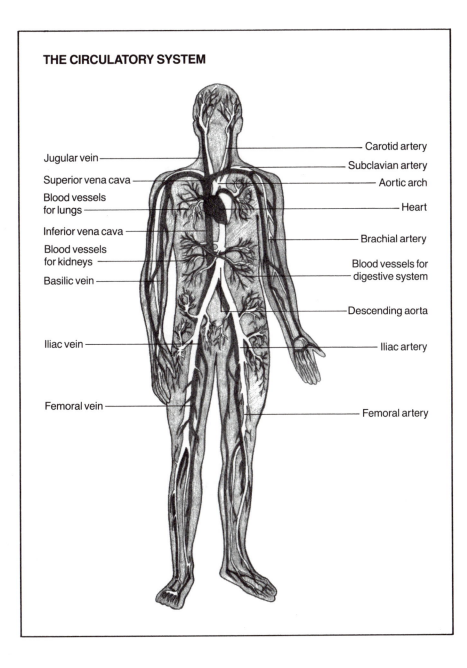

Jugular vein

Superior vena cava

Blood vessels for lungs

Inferior vena cava

Blood vessels for kidneys

Basilic vein

Iliac vein

Femoral vein

Carotid artery

Subclavian artery

Aortic arch

Heart

Brachial artery

Blood vessels for digestive system

Descending aorta

Iliac artery

Femoral artery

In this wall painting of an embalming, Anubis, the dog-headed Egyptian god of the underworld, supervises the preparation of the body. The figure with wings represents the soul of the dead, waiting to be reunited with the body. Because the embalmers actually removed the organs from the body as part of the embalming process, they were familiar with the internal parts.

the body. Thus, more than thirty-six hundred years ago, Egyptian doctors knew that vessels led from the heart to all parts of the body. They didn't know, however, that blood moved through those vessels, and they didn't understand the heart's purpose—most of them thought that *it* was where a person's thoughts and feelings came from. In other words, they thought that the heart did what the brain actually does.

Doctors in India, about twenty-three hundred years ago, believed that seven hundred blood vessels began somewhere near the stomach and ran to all parts of the body. They thought that blood was produced in the intestines and that it eventually turned into flesh! Of course, they were at a disadvantage, because they were forbidden by their religion to examine a dead body. They had to get most of their information simply by looking at the outsides of live people, unless they happened to be able to see some of the insides of a person who had been injured.

In Europe, the study of the heart and blood began, as many things did, in ancient Greece. The Greeks were the greatest scientists of the ancient world. They were interested in everything and wanted to know the causes and reasons for anything that happened, whether an eclipse of the sun or a sudden attack of illness. It was ancient Greek scientists who figured out that Earth is a sphere, worked out the existence of atoms, came up with a theory of evolution, and produced what scientists now call the law of conservation of energy, a thousand years and more before other European peoples even thought about such things.

The ancient Greeks did not live only in the land we call Greece today; they were spread out in a great many parts of the Mediterranean area. Between 700 and 500 B.C., they established colonies along the shores of what are now Iran and Turkey, and on islands in the Aegean and Mediterranean seas. In the fourth century B.C., Greeks and Macedonians (people of a land adjoining Greece) conquered the Persian Empire, which covered what are now Iran, Iraq, Turkey, Israel, Syria, Egypt, Libya, and parts of

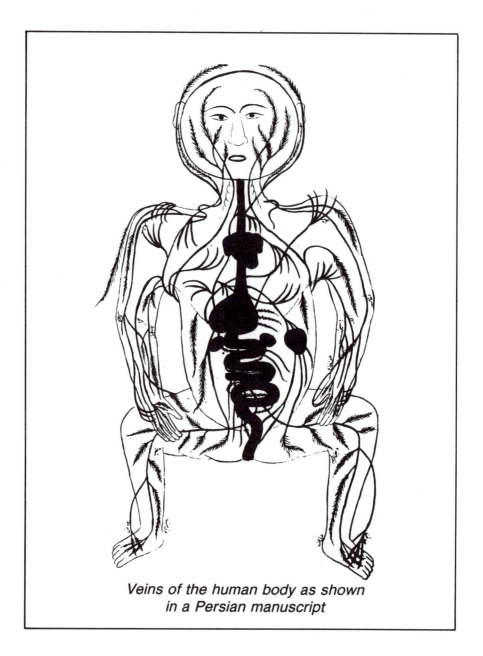

*Veins of the human body as shown
in a Persian manuscript*

Russia and Afghanistan. They eventually moved into all these areas, spreading their ideas and ways of doing things. All the places where Greeks lived and ruled formed a single great community throughout which science, including the study of the human body, flourished.

One of the first Greek scientists we know of who gave special thought to the heart and blood was a man known as Empedocles of Akragas, who lived in the fifth century B.C. He believed that the heart controlled the blood and that the blood flowed in and out of the heart, but, like the Egyptians, he didn't realize that blood flowed through the vessels that led to and from the heart. He thought that a special kind of air, called *pneuma*, flowed through these tubes to all parts of the body. Empedocles thought that *pneuma* was taken in with ordinary air when a person breathed, but the body separated it out and made use of it to stay alive. So, while some of his ideas were right, others were wrong.

Another Greek, who lived at about the same time as Empedocles, was the man who set the standards that doctors follow to this day. His name was Hippocrates, and he is regarded as the father of modern medical science and practice.

Hippocrates believed that it should be possible to discover how the human body, or anything else in the universe, worked by simply studying the known facts about it and then using logic to figure out the meaning of the facts. Using this method, he proved to himself that diseases had only natural causes and were not the result of demons, curses, spirits, or any other supernatural things, as most people then believed. He discovered cures and treatments for a number of diseases and kinds of injuries, and he performed successful operations. However, like Empedocles, he did not really understand how the circulatory system worked. He, too, thought it was air that moved through a body's arteries and veins.

The trouble was that Hippocrates, Empedocles, and other Greek doctors of that time were in the same situation as the ancient Indian doctors: They were never able to see inside a

In this woodcut, Hippocrates is
dissecting a bull's head.

human body as the Egyptian doctors had been able to do. The Greeks, too, believed that a human body was sacred and should not be cut up for any reason. Thus, Hippocrates and the others had to get most of their information from the bodies of animals and birds that were cut up for food.

However, by some seventy-five years after the time of Hippocrates, things had changed, and Greek doctors were allowed to dissect (cut up) human corpses in order to learn from them. One of the first to do this was a man known as Herophilus of Chalcedon, who studied the insides of human bodies very carefully and made a number of important discoveries.

Herophilus was the first to notice that there is a clear difference between arteries and veins. He pointed out that arteries were about six times as thick as veins. He was also the first Greek to determine that it is blood, not air, that runs through veins. He found that there seemed to be a connection between the beating of the heart and the pulse that can be felt by pressing an artery, and he came to believe that a strong pulse was the sign of a strong heart. Thus, Herophilus provided some correct, important information about the circulatory system.

A few years later, a Greek doctor known as Erasistratus of Chios noted that every organ in a human body had both a vein and artery leading to it. He agreed with Herophilus that veins carried blood, but he still believed that arteries carried air. It seemed to him that the veins and arteries must be connected in some way, although he could not see any such connections.

And so, by around twenty-three hundred years ago, most Greek doctors and scientists thought that blood flowed only through a body's veins and that the flow of the blood was controlled in some way by the heart. But they had no idea what blood did or what it was for, and they had some strange ideas about what the heart could do—such as their belief that it could turn ordinary air from the lungs into magical *pneuma*, which was then sent out through the arteries to keep the body alive. They were

THE "SPIRIT" THEORY OF ERASISTRATUS

Erasistratus of Chios (c. 290 B.C.) believed that air passed from the lungs to the heart where it was changed into a "vital spirit," which traveled through the arteries to various parts of the body. In the brain the vital spirit became the "animal spirit," which reached the organs of the body through hollow nerves.

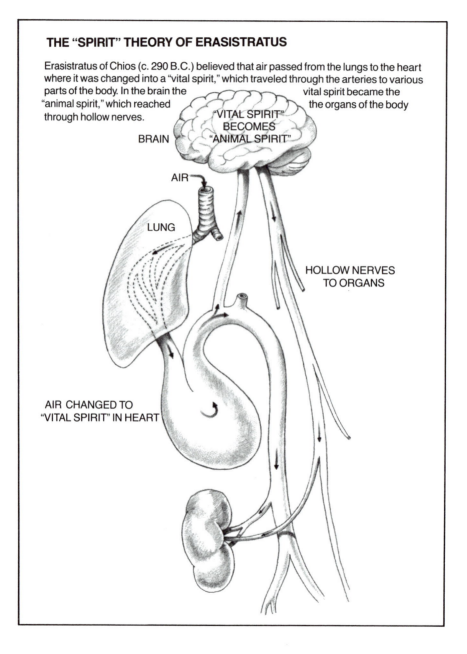

BRAIN

"VITAL SPIRIT"
BECOMES
"ANIMAL SPIRIT"

AIR

LUNG

HOLLOW NERVES
TO ORGANS

AIR CHANGED TO
"VITAL SPIRIT" IN HEART

still a long way from understanding the real work of the heart and blood, although they were far closer than the Egyptians had been, and closer than the Indians or any other ancient peoples of their time.

The reason why the Greeks didn't do better at finding out exactly how the heart and blood work was their belief that they could figure things out just by looking at and thinking about them. Few if any Greek scientists seem ever to have thought about trying to see if what they had figured out was really true. They simply accepted what seemed to be logical. They all accepted the idea of pneuma, although no one had ever tried to find out if there really was such a thing. They just didn't think that way.

By the third century B.C., the Greek world had lost most of its vigor, and it was easily conquered by the Romans. However, the Romans were slightly in awe of the Greeks, whose art, science, and culture were a good deal better than anything the Romans had. So, instead of wiping out the Greek culture and replacing it with their own, as conquerors generally do, the Romans carefully preserved Greek culture and ideas and took them over as their own. Thus, for the next few hundred years, it was still Greek scientists and doctors who did most of the investigating into how the human body worked. And it was a Greek doctor living in Rome who finally came up with an idea about the way the circulatory system worked, an idea that was accepted by people for the next fourteen hundred years.

CHAPTER

2

THE IDEA THAT LASTED FOURTEEN CENTURIES

About A.D. 130 a boy was born in the town of Pergamum, which is now the city of Bergama, Turkey. His father, a well-known and respected Greek architect, named the boy Galenos, a Greek name meaning "calm" or "serene." The boy grew up to become a famous doctor who is known to us today as Galen, and who is regarded as one of the great leaders in the history of medical science.

Galen was born a citizen of the Roman Empire, which extended over most of what is now Western Europe, the Middle East, and North Africa. It was ruled, at the time of Galen's birth, by the emperor Hadrian, a good ruler who worked hard to keep the empire at peace and to make its government more efficient. Galen grew up in a world of law and order, peace and security.

Life was not at all primitive in the larger, older cities of the empire. Most of them had stone-paved streets with underground sewers, and some even had street lights, lanterns that were hung out at night. There were shops, schools, theaters, public parks, and places of amusement. Almost every city with a large Greek population, such as Pergamum, had a gymnasium, where people could go to exercise and take part in athletic contests. There was a police force to look after things, and many people made their living by taking care of the needs of others—people such as clothes cleaners, barbers, bankers, and, of course, doctors.

At the time when Rome conquered the Greek world, Roman medical science did not even exist. For the most part, Romans who were ill simply tried to cure themselves, using concoctions made from plants, magical charms and chants, and prayers. Seeing such a wide-open field, numbers of Greek doctors began moving to Rome and other Roman cities, and before long, Greek ideas about health and medicine were standard throughout the empire. By the time Galen was born, medical science had reached a fairly high state. Doctors were thoroughly familiar with hundreds of diseases and conditions and had medicines for treating them, and they could also perform a good many different kinds of operations, using many kinds of surgical instruments that are still used today. They apparently even had a kind of anesthetic—a drink made from a plant root—which put people to sleep for operations. However, doctors' knowledge of what went on inside the human body was still rather poor, and they still had no idea of how the circulatory system worked—or that there even *was* such a thing as the circulatory system.

Medical science was of considerable importance in Galen's birthplace. The city of Pergamum had a temple of the Greek and Roman god of healing, Asclepius, with a medical school attached. Perhaps this had something to do with Galen's decision to become a doctor. At any rate Galen's father was wealthy enough to provide his son with a good education, and at the age of seventeen Galen entered the Pergamum medical school, known as the Asclepieion. From there, his father sent him on to study at the great educational centers—Smyrna, in what is now Turkey; Corinth, in Greece; and Alexandria, Egypt, which was the main center of Greek culture, having a university, a museum, and the world's largest library. During his five years in Alexandria, Galen began dissecting animals to study the workings of their inner organs.

In the year 157, at the age of twenty-seven, Galen returned

home to Pergamum as a full-fledged doctor. Like most of the cities in the Roman Empire, Pergamum had a stadium in which "games" were held—mostly actual battles by men known as gladiators, who fought against each other with swords and spears and often fought dangerous wild animals as well, for the entertainment of the audiences who came to see them. Naturally, some of these men received serious wounds and injuries, so a full-time doctor was needed to take care of them. Galen was appointed official physician of the Pergamum stadium soon after his return. This was extremely helpful to him, because one of his main interests was to find out the purpose of every part of the human body, and caring for wounded gladiators could help him do this. Dissection of dead people was forbidden by Roman law, and although doctors could dissect animals, it wasn't as valuable as being able to see what was inside a human body. But now, Galen had frequent chances to see the inside parts of men who had been cut open during battles.

At the age of thirty-three, Galen left Pergamum again and went to Rome, the capital of the empire, to seek his fortune. The emperor was Marcus Aurelius, a sensitive and intelligent man who believed people should be free to think as they pleased and to seek knowledge. Thus, there was a spirit of freedom and curiosity in Rome, and a bright, curious person such as Galen fit right in.

He was quickly recognized as a highly competent and skillful doctor. He was able to cure a famed and respected philosopher, named Eudemus, of a troublesome condition, and Eudemus began recommending Galen to his friends, all of whom were wealthy and important people. Galen was generally willing to try to cure patients whom most other doctors had given up on, and because he was often successful, his reputation grew. In time, he was appointed official physician to the emperor himself and to the emperor's son, Commodus.

Such success made Galen wealthy, and that made him free to devote more time to the study of the human body. He still could

Galen, the figure in the middle, gives a lecture on the heart. The philosopher Aristotle is on the left.

GALEN'S THEORY ON THE CIRCULATION OF THE BLOOD

Claudius Galen (c. 150-c.200), physician to the emperors of Rome, propounded a complex and totally erroneous system of circulation, which confused physicians for centuries.

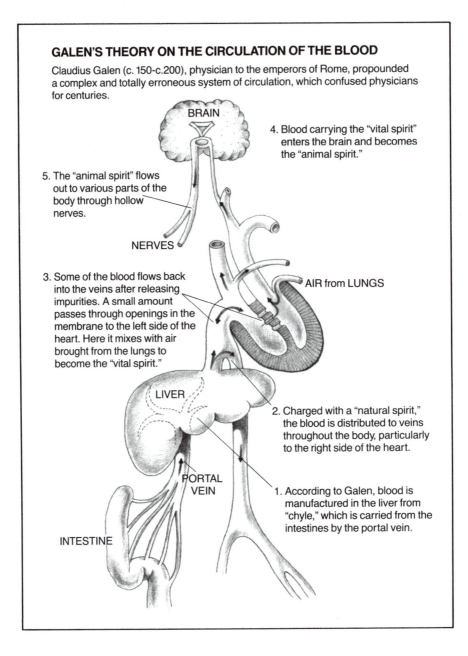

BRAIN

4. Blood carrying the "vital spirit" enters the brain and becomes the "animal spirit."

5. The "animal spirit" flows out to various parts of the body through hollow nerves.

NERVES

3. Some of the blood flows back into the veins after releasing impurities. A small amount passes through openings in the membrane to the left side of the heart. Here it mixes with air brought from the lungs to become the "vital spirit."

AIR from LUNGS

LIVER

2. Charged with a "natural spirit," the blood is distributed to veins throughout the body, particularly to the right side of the heart.

PORTAL VEIN

1. According to Galen, blood is manufactured in the liver from "chyle," which is carried from the intestines by the portal vein.

INTESTINE

not dissect humans, of course, so he began to work with apes brought from Africa, because they seemed to him to be very much like humans. And gradually, from his dissections of apes and other animals, and his observations of how their inside parts seemed to work, he built up an idea about the functioning of the heart and blood that was different in many ways from the ideas of Hippocrates and the other Greek doctors who had worked on the problem in the past.

For one thing, it seemed to Galen as if the *liver* was actually the center of the system of arteries, veins, and blood. It was easy for him to get such an idea, because the liver contains a treelike tangle of veins and arteries that look as if they all lead out of it, and it is filled with blood that oozes out of it when it is cut.

But the liver actually has nothing to do with the circulation of blood. It is the body's chemical laboratory, food storehouse, and center for the control of any poisons, pollution, or pests—disease-causing bacteria—that get into the body. The human liver is a very large organ located just under the lungs and above the stomach. Blood coming from the heart flows into it through a large artery that branches out into many thousands of vessels reaching into all parts of the liver. Blood going back to the heart comes into the liver through a vein leading from the small intestine. This blood contains waste from the body's cells, digested food particles from the intestine, and things that have come into the body from outside, such as chemicals and bacteria. The liver removes most of the waste products, changes them into several kinds of chemicals, and sends them off to the kidneys to be flushed out of the body in water. It picks up all food particles and turns them into a starchy substance that it stores up to be sent out when needed. It removes harmful bacteria from the blood and brings in some of the body's "security" cells to get rid of them by eating them. It produces chemicals that it sends to the intestine to help with the digestion of food, and it does several other things as well. So, though it is a very important organ, it is not part of the circulatory system.

Galen, however, felt sure that it was. He thought that the liver actually *made* blood, filled it with food and a sort of magical "charge," and sent it to the heart. There is a milky liquid called *chyle*, containing digested fat, which flows out of the small intestine into the liver, and Galen thought that the liver turned this into blood. Like most of the ancient Greek doctors, as well as the doctors of his own time, Galen still believed in pneuma, the sort of magical substance in air, and he thought the liver put pneuma into the blood it made, along with dissolved food from the intestine, and then sent the blood into the veins. He did not think that the liver pumped the blood, however, but that the blood simply ebbed and flowed through the veins.

In time, according to Galen, the blood flowed into the right side of the heart, and there the impurities it had picked up from the body were sent out through an artery into the lungs and were exhaled out of the body. The blood, now clean, oozed back into the veins, but some of it flowed through tiny holes in the septum—the wall between the two parts of the heart—and went into the heart's left chamber. There, it became mixed with air that had come from the lungs, and this air, according to Galen's beliefs, was filled with pneuma that became mixed with the blood, turning it into a rather magical liquid that flowed out into the arteries and was taken up to the brain. In the brain the blood was changed again, into what Galen called *animal spirit*, which was then carried by the nerves to all parts of the body to keep the body alive.

These were Galen's beliefs about the blood, the heart, and the liver—a mixture of magic, guesswork, and a few actual facts. He was mostly wrong, but he *had* made several important discoveries. He was the first person to realize that blood, not air, was in the arteries. And although he couldn't see the capillaries that connect arteries to veins, he felt sure that veins and arteries must be connected in some way, and that blood passed from one to the other. Perhaps this should have made him realize that blood must flow in a continuous circle, but it apparently never occurred to him.

Galen was really quite a good doctor and a true scientist in his studies of the human body. He wrote more than four hundred books, many of which still exist, that included information on diseases, bones, muscles, and surgery, as well as on the organs of the body and their work. He was regarded by most of the people of his own time as a very great and wise man, and he is regarded today as one of the great scholars in the field of medical science.

But, like the Greek doctors before him, Galen depended mainly on *reasoning* to figure things out, and he did little if anything to try to find out if what he had reasoned was correct. Thus, most of his explanations of how the body and its organs work, like his explanation of the circulatory system, were full of errors. However, because of his reputation and fame, these error-filled explanations were accepted as the absolute truth for the next fourteen hundred years.

CHAPTER

3

MARKING TIME

The Roman Empire was at the height of its power during Galen's lifetime, but soon after his death it began slipping downhill. Many times during the next hundred years, men of wealth and power simply seized the position of emperor, and there were civil wars. This enabled barbarian Germanic tribes—the Goths, Visigoths, and Ostrogoths—to begin pushing into Roman territory in Europe, and the rising new Persian Empire began taking over Roman territory in the Near East. In the year 410 an army of Visigoths pushed all the way to the city of Rome itself, broke into the city and looted it, and then marched away. In 476 the last official Roman emperor, a frightened twelve-year-old boy, was forced to give up the throne to a German chieftain. Other chieftains began grabbing up pieces of Roman territory, and soon Europe was broken up into a number of little barbarian kingdoms that were generally quarreling and fighting with one another. The law, order, and civilization that had been kept up by the Roman Empire were gone, and what is sometimes known as the Dark Ages had begun.

For most people life now consisted of little more than trying to grow enough food to keep from starving and often having to fight to protect what they had from bandits or enemy warriors. There were no longer any such things as universities, medical schools, or museums and libraries, and the study of science, including medical science, was simply forgotten. There were no longer any doctors, either, and people who became ill or injured tried to heal themselves with magical spells or prayer.

However, the ideas, discoveries, and knowledge of men such as Hippocrates and Galen were not lost. Before the Roman Empire fell apart, Christianity had become its official religion, so when the Dark Ages began, there were many monasteries and church buildings scattered throughout the parts of Europe that had been Roman territory. In many of these places copies of the writings of famous Greek and Roman men of wisdom had been carefully preserved. Copies of many such books had also been preserved in parts of the Near East that had once belonged to Rome, and it was in the Near East that the study of medical science began once more.

Things were not quite as bad in the Near East as they were in Europe. In the 600s the Muslims, followers of the religious leader Muhammad, grew in power in Arabia and came sweeping out to conquer what are now Syria, Lebanon, Jordan, Israel, Iraq, Iran, and Egypt. Most of the people in those countries became Muslims, and in time most of them were also speaking the Arabic language, so a united empire was formed. It was not as well organized as the Roman Empire, but it did provide law and order and saw to the building of such things as schools, universities, and even hospitals. Thus, there were soon capable doctors and scholars of medical science throughout the Near East.

Much of what these doctors and scholars knew and believed was based on Galen's writings. They thought of him as the greatest authority on medical science and had no doubt that everything he said was absolutely correct. Thus, like Galen, they believed that blood was created in the liver and sent to the heart to be purified. In the 1200s a well-known Arabian doctor, Ibn al-Nafis, did disagree with Galen's statement that blood passed from the right part of the heart to the left part through tiny openings in the septum, because Ibn al-Nafis didn't think there were any such openings; but even so he and all the other Muslim doctors continued to believe in Galen.

In Europe things gradually got better, and life became easier for most people. By the 1300s there were many large cities with universities, men were studying the work of Galen and other Greek and Roman scholars, and there were again doctors. But in Europe, too, there was a feeling that Galen was simply the last word in medical knowledge. Because the Christian Church had preserved Galen's work, it was almost as if a person could not doubt Galen without doubting the Church as well, and so Galen's ideas about the work of the heart, blood, and everything else, were accepted without question. A famous and highly respected teacher of the medical school of the University of Paris declared that it would be impossible to learn anything more about the human body than Galen knew!

It was not until the 1500s, fourteen centuries after Galen's time, that a few doctors began to wonder about some of Galen's statements and beliefs. One of these men was a Belgian, Andreas Vesalius, who became one of the most famous medical scientists of his time and who is regarded today as the man who started the modern science of anatomy, the study of the human body.

Vesalius was born in 1514, into a family whose men for three generations had been doctors. As a young boy he was tremendously interested in anatomy and dissected the bodies of dead birds, mice, and other small animals. At the age of seventeen he went to the medical school of the University of Paris to study medicine and, in particular, anatomy.

The way anatomy was taught at that time was for the professor to sit on a chair on a raised platform, high above the class, and simply to read from one of Galen's books on anatomy. As he read, an assistant would dissect a corpse—generally, the body of a criminal who had been hanged or put to death in some other way. As the professor described a particular organ, muscle, or

The sixteenth-century anatomist Andreas Vesalius gives an anatomy lesson using an actual human body, an innovative procedure at that time. Behind the body is a symbol of death, the skeleton of a man holding a scythe, the so-called Grim Reaper.

other part, the assistant would point to the part so that the students clustered around him could see what was being described. Students could ask questions—as long as their questions didn't challenge any of Galen's statements or argue with his beliefs.

Vesalius didn't care for this kind of instruction. He wanted to find the parts of the body for himself and see them up close. Taking some terrible chances, he actually stole several bodies and performed dissections. He would read from Galen's books as he worked, but if he found something that didn't seem to be the way Galen had described it, he would simply assume that Galen had been wrong—which would have infuriated most of Vesalius's teachers!

In time Vesalius became quite a famous doctor and professor of anatomy and wrote a series of books on parts of the human body. In one of these books he discussed the work of the heart and blood. Like Ibn al-Nafis, of whom he had never heard, Vesalius believed that Galen was completely wrong about the idea that blood got from the right side of the heart to the left side by oozing through openings in the septum. Vesalius pointed out that no such opening could be seen. He also found a great many other things wrong with Galen's statements and ideas about the human body, and he discussed these in his books. He was bitterly opposed by a number of other doctors and anatomists, who were furious that he had the nerve to disagree with the great Galen.

At about the same time Vesalius was writing his books, another man was also writing a book that strongly contradicted some of Galen's statements. This was a strange sort of "part-

Andreas Vesalius is using a cadaver to demonstrate how the muscles in the arms and hands function.

AN. ÆT. XXVII   M D XLII

time" doctor known as Michael Servetus. Servetus studied medicine and anatomy at the University of Paris, but he also spent a great deal of time studying and writing about religion. Some of the things he put into his religious books got him into a great deal of trouble, for they challenged the major teachings of both the Catholic and Protestant churches, which was considered a crime in those days. Eventually, Servetus was seized, clapped into jail and burned at the stake.

However, in the last book he wrote before his capture and execution, Servetus showed that he had made a major discovery about blood. He, too, refused to believe Galen's claim that blood oozed from the right part of the heart to the left through openings in the septum, and he also rejected Galen's belief that blood went into the lungs merely to bring them nutrition. Servetus said that blood traveled *through* the lungs in order to pick up "vital spirits," and then, filled with these spirits, it went into the left part of the heart and on into the body's arteries. This is exactly right, of course, except that blood doesn't pick up "vital spirits," it picks up oxygen. However, the word *oxygen* didn't even exist in Servetus's time, and people didn't know there was such a thing as gas, which is what oxygen is. But Servetus was certainly on the right track; he knew there was something in the air that was inhaled into the lungs and that was picked up by the blood and carried through the body.

Michael Servetus had actually discovered what is now called the "lesser circulation" of blood, which was really only one step away from discovering the whole system of blood circulation. But absolutely nothing came of this discovery at that time, for not only was Servetus burned but so were all his books, except for a few that managed to survive because they were tucked away in forgotten places. So, few if any other doctors ever learned of his discovery. (Chances are they wouldn't have believed it anyway.)

However, in 1559 a book written by an Italian professor of anatomy named Realdo Colombo, published after Colombo's death, showed that he had made the same discovery as Servetus but had gone a good deal deeper into it. Colombo also made some sharp criticisms of Galen's ideas. Inasmuch as he was a respected professor, other medical scholars paid a great deal more attention to his ideas than they would have paid to those of Servetus.

A little before Servetus and Colombo had made their discovery of lesser circulation, another Italian professor of anatomy, Giovanni Canano, had also made an important discovery. He found something that had not been noticed by Galen or anyone else—that certain veins have *valves*.

A valve is a movable flap or disk that is put into water pipes, gas pipes, faucets, and so on, to control the flow of liquid or gas through them, and some veins have folds in their inside surfaces that act as valves. As blood flows steadily through the veins the folds lie flat, allowing the blood to keep moving forward. But if something, such as a cut in the vein, causes pressure to get weak so that blood in the vein is not being pushed forward by the blood behind it, the folds lift up, blocking the vein so that blood that has moved past the valves cannot begin to back up and flow the wrong way.

Canano's discovery of valves in veins probably should have made him realize that blood is meant to flow steadily in one direction, rather than ebbing and flowing as Galen had thought. Perhaps Canano did realize the truth, but if so, he never said anything about it—probably because he did not want to contradict Galen. And many years later, in 1603, when still another famous Italian professor of anatomy, Girolamo Fabrici, produced a small book about veins, he worked out an explanation for valves that made them fit into Galen's ideas. He said that the main purposes of valves was simply to keep veins from getting too full of blood that was rushing eagerly to get to places where it was needed. He also believed that valves probably closed up at times in order to make sure that all nearby parts of the body got enough blood before the blood was allowed to go rushing on its way.

Thus, by the second half of the 1500s, while most medical scholars and doctors still swore by Galen's ideas and statements, a number of them felt that Galen might have been wrong about a lot of things, although they weren't quite ready to suggest that he might have been wrong about most things. But all the facts were now available to figure out exactly how the heart and blood really worked. It was known that blood moved from the right side of the heart into the lungs, that there were valves in veins, that the blood in veins was a different color from the blood in arteries, and so on. It needed only one person to break completely free of all Galen's ideas and put the facts together correctly.

That person was born in England in 1578. His name was William Harvey.

Sketches drawn by Leonardo da Vinci, showing anatomical makeup of the heart. Leonardo stole cadavers to dissect so that he could render anatomical features in his art with perfect accuracy.

4

HARVEY SOLVES
THE PUZZLE

England today is united with Scotland, Wales, and Northern Ireland, forming the United Kingdom, which is associated with some fifty other countries in an organization known as the Commonwealth of Nations. But in Harvey's time, England was united only with little Wales. So, unlike Galen, who was born into a mighty empire, Harvey was born into a tiny kingdom about the size of the state of Alabama. It was ruled by a queen named Elizabeth (Elizabeth I).

However, the world that Harvey grew up in was very much like the world Galen had known, for there had really been very few changes in fourteen centuries. Most of the people of England were farmers or shepherds who lived and worked almost exactly as Roman farmers and shepherds had, fourteen hundred years before. Houses were lighted by candles and heated by open fireplaces; land travel was accomplished by riding on horseback, riding in a horse-drawn carriage or wagon, or just walking; and clothing, tools, and most other things were still made by hand. Wars were still fought mainly by soldiers wearing armor and carrying swords and spears, although some now carried firearms or fired cannon, neither of which had existed in Galen's time. But the inventions of gunpowder and the printing press were actually about the only main differences between Harvey's world and Galen's. The doctors of Harvey's time had no more instruments or knowledge than those of Galen's time; generally, in fact, they had less. Most of what they knew and believed was still based on what Galen had known and believed.

This was true in other fields, too. Just as Galen was the last word in medical science, a Greek called Ptolemy, who had lived at about the same time as Galen, was regarded as the last word in astronomy, and a Roman called Pliny was the last word in natural science. The things these men had written were not to be doubted any more than what Galen had written was to be doubted. But, just as a few doctors and medical scholars had begun to question Galen's statements, people in other fields were beginning to question the wisdom of Ptolemy, Pliny, and the other ancients. And, thirty years before Harvey was born, something happened that was to lead to the eventual destruction of the last bits of blind faith in the ancients and the start of a new way of thinking that was to influence Harvey deeply.

What happened was that a Polish astronomer called Nicolaus Copernicus wrote a book that shattered an idea which, like Galen's, had been accepted without question for fourteen centuries. This was Ptolemy's idea that our world was the center of the universe, that it was fixed in place and did not move, and that everything else—the sun, stars, and planets—moved around it. Copernicus proved that this was all completely wrong. With mathematics, diagrams, and logical arguments, he showed that the Earth is a mere planet that goes around the sun with all the other planets. He also showed that the universe is tremendously bigger than Ptolemy had believed, and that the stars are fantastically far away.

Copernicus's book truly started what is sometimes known as the scientific revolution. It caused people to begin thinking about things in a completely different way. It meant that instead of just accepting ideas and beliefs because everyone else accepted them, or because you were told to accept them, a person could question them and perhaps think of ways to prove that they were wrong. Proving things instead of accepting them—that was the new idea stirring in Europe, and especially in England, as William Harvey grew up.

Harvey's father was a prosperous farmer and landowner who also became a successful merchant, so he was able to see to it that William, his eldest son, received a good education. At the age of fifteen the boy was sent to an English college where he studied medicine and related subjects. On his graduation, in 1599, his father sent him on to the finest medical school in Europe at that time, the University of Padua, in Italy.

Padua was not only a good medical school, it was a good school for many other fields as well. One of the professors who was teaching mathematics and astronomy while Harvey was there was Galileo Galilei, the man who is now regarded as the founder of modern experimental science. Galileo was famous even then, and thousands of students went to Padua simply because he was a teacher there. He was an enthusiastic supporter of Copernicus's ideas and a strong believer in performing experiments to find things out. Even though William Harvey was in another field he must have often heard, from other students, of Galileo's ideas and methods.

Harvey spent two and a half years at the University of Padua and was an outstanding student. But it seems apparent that he quickly realized there was a great deal that wasn't known about such things as the work of the heart and blood and that no one was making any real effort to find out about them.

He received his diploma as a doctor and returned to England. He had to take several examinations in order to practice medicine in England, but by 1604 he was licensed to practice in the city of London. He married Elizabeth Browne, the daughter of the man who was physician to the king, James I, and they set up house-keeping not far from the College of Physicians in London.

The new way of thinking that had been sparked by Copernicus and developed by Galileo was spreading through London

The young William Harvey

about this time. William Gilbert, who had been King James's doctor before Harvey's father-in-law, had spent several years doing experiments with magnetism, and he had put his discoveries into a book that was being widely read—the first book ever written from the viewpoint of modern science. A member of Parliament, Sir Francis Bacon, had just finished writing a book called *The Advancement of Learning*, in which he advised people to ignore the beliefs of such ancient wisdom seekers as Galen and Ptolemy and to investigate things for themselves and perform experiments to prove the truth of what they believed.

Exciting things were happening throughout the rest of Europe as well. In his theory about the movement of Earth and the other planets, Copernicus had said that they moved in circles around the sun, but this did not seem to work out well mathematically, and many people were able to challenge Copernicus's whole idea because of that detail. However, in 1609 the German astronomer Johannes Kepler figured out that the planets actually move in ellipses, or ovals, rather than circles. Mathematically, this worked out perfectly and proved that Copernicus had been right. Then, in 1610, using a telescope he had built himself, Galileo discovered four moons circling the planet Jupiter. This added more proof to Copernicus's theory. These discoveries of Kepler and Galileo, like those of Gilbert and a few other men of that time, showed that people could, indeed, discover new, unsuspected things by using the new scientific methods suggested by Francis Bacon.

William Harvey surely heard about all these discoveries and ideas, and they must have made an impression on him. Sir Francis Bacon became one of Dr. Harvey's patients, and Bacon's beliefs must have been well known to Harvey. On the other hand, Harvey was an intelligent, alert man, and what he did he may have done entirely on his own, with no "input" from the ideas or methods of anyone else. At any rate, apparently in the years 1609 to 1616, using modern scientific methods, Dr. William Harvey discovered the circulatory system—the actual work of the heart and blood.

In order to find out what he wanted to know about the heart and blood, Harvey, like some other doctors and anatomists of his time and many afterward, made use of vivisection—he cut open the bodies of living animals such as toads, fish, snails, crabs, and others—so that he could watch what living hearts did. But for a long time he despaired of ever being able to find anything out, for the movements of the hearts of most of these creatures were so quick and hard to follow that Harvey couldn't make out what was going on.

Finally, things began to fall into place, and he became able to understand what was happening. He began to realize what a "heartbeat" was—the heart lay quietly, then it drew itself together, then it suddenly expanded outward with a force that made it lift up, then it fell back to lie quietly again. Harvey noticed that it was a deep red in color when it lay quiet, but it turned pale as it moved. He touched beating hearts and felt them grow hard as they squeezed together and soft as they relaxed. And in time, from all this, Harvey realized that the heart was a pump. When it lay quiet, it was dark red because it was filling up with blood that was coming into it from the lungs. When it pulled itself together and grew hard, it was squeezing all this blood out of itself, and it became pale when all the blood was squeezed out. Furthermore, Harvey saw that when the main artery leading out of the heart was cut, blood *spurted* out of it, with the spurts coming at the exact moments the heart completed one of its pumping actions. Obviously, the heart was pumping blood into the arteries.

So the heart was a pump, steadily pumping blood. But Harvey wanted to know where all this blood was going. And where was all the blood that entered the heart coming from?

To try to find out, Harvey did something that no other doctor or anatomist had ever thought of doing. He estimated the amount of blood that the heart pumped out each time it beat and multiplied that by the number of times a heart beat during half an hour. This showed him that more blood passed through a heart in a short period of time than could possibly be manufactured in the liver, as Galen had thought. In fact, it was even more blood than could be held in all the veins and arteries at one time.

It seemed to Harvey that this showed there must be a fixed, or unchanging, amount of blood in a body, and that it simply moved through the heart over and over. He decided that blood had to be moving in a kind of circle, and that it must flow from the heart into the arteries, from the arteries into the veins, and from the veins back into the heart.

This was easy to prove. Harvey knew that if an animal's main artery was cut open, so that blood flowed steadily out of it, within a short time the animal's body would be completely empty of blood. There would be no blood in either its arteries or veins. This could only happen because the fixed amount of blood in the body had been allowed to leak out and wasn't able to complete its journey from arteries into veins. Furthermore, Harvey determined that the valves in the veins would only allow the blood to flow in one direction—toward the heart. Simple logic indicated that this was the way it was *supposed* to flow.

By 1616 there was no doubt in Harvey's mind. By that time he had been appointed a teacher at the College of Physicians, and in the lectures he gave, he told his students as a matter of *fact* that there was "a perpetual [continuous] motion of the blood in a circle, caused by the pulsation of the heart."

However, it wasn't until the year 1628 that Harvey announced his discovery. That year he had a small book published in Frankfurt, Germany, which described his experiments and presented his arguments. The book was written in Latin, so that it could be read and understood by doctors of all the European nations, most of whom could read Latin no matter what their native language was. The title of the book (translated) was *Anatomical Exercises on the Motion of the Heart and Blood in Animals*.

*Harvey using an animal to demonstrate
the circulation of the blood*

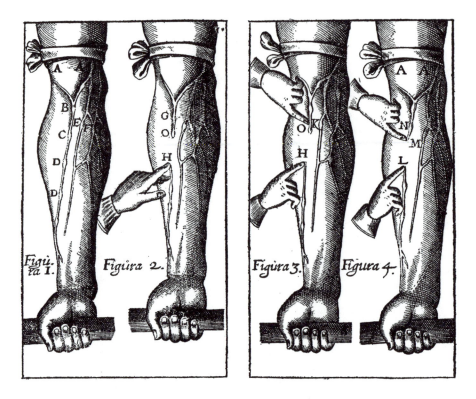

Harvey's Anatomical Exercises on the Motion of the Heart and Blood in Animals *made use of illustrations to demonstrate his contentions about the circulation of the blood.*

Harvey's book was published at a time when there was a great deal of opposition to the new ways of science. Church leaders had come to realize that what Copernicus had said about the movement of the earth and the size of the universe conflicted with some parts of the Bible, and so they had banned his book. In 1600 an Italian philosopher, Giordano Bruno, who had publicly proclaimed his belief in Copernicus's work and the new science, had been tried for heresy by the Catholic Church and burned at the stake. Church leaders were also angry at Galileo, because he had published reports of his discoveries of Jupiter's moons and of sunspots, and he had been warned not to continue his support of Copernicus's work. Many teachers, doctors, philosophers, and others in various fields of science agreed with the Church, refusing to accept the new ways of science, and refusing to believe that the ancients such as Galen and Ptolemy could have been wrong.

Of course, most of what Harvey had discovered completely contradicted things Galen had said, and Harvey's book caused a storm of angry protest. A famous scholar and physician, James Primrose, wrote a booklet entitled *Against the Thesis of Harvey*, in which he provided many arguments attempting to show that Harvey was wrong. Many leading doctors in France, Germany, Austria, and Italy scoffed at Harvey's ideas.

Harvey had known this was going to happen. In the chapter of his book in which he talked about the actual circulation of the blood, he began by saying that what he was going to reveal was "so strange and undreamed of, that not only do I fear danger to myself from the malice of a few, but I dread lest I have all men as my enemies. . . ." However, he then went on to say, "My hope is in the love of truth and the integrity of intelligence." In other words, having found out the truth he felt it was absolutely essential to let everyone know it, and he was counting on the belief that enough other scientists would see the truth of what he had told them and would stand up for it.

But things went rather badly for him for a time. He had been appointed royal physician to King Charles I in 1618, and the king backed him, but many of Dr. Harvey's other patients left him. Harvey sadly told a friend that most people thought he was "crack-brained" and that most other doctors were against him.

Then things began to swing the other way. The famous French philosopher-scientist René Descartes, who invented the form of mathematics called analytic geometry, came out on Harvey's side. So did the king of France. A number of important doc-

tors and anatomists who had been against Harvey began to change their minds and agree with him. In time, Harvey's description of the circulatory system was being taught as fact at all the universities of Europe.

Harvey's discovery of the circulatory system was a major breakthrough, as important as Copernicus's discovery of the motion of the earth had been. It wiped out thousands of years of guesswork, nonsense, and unquestioning belief, and replaced them with real knowledge. It opened up many possibilities for new ways of curing people and saving lives, for once doctors knew how the heart and blood really worked, they began to figure out such things as tourniquets to stop the flow of blood, transfusions to save the lives of people who had lost too much blood, and so on. Thus, Harvey's discovery also showed the importance of science in providing facts that could be put to use.

In doing his work with the heart and blood, Harvey was no better equipped than Vesalius, Colombo, or any of the other doctors or anatomists who had studied the heart before him. He was really not even any better equipped than Galen had been, despite the passage of fourteen hundred years. Any of those men could have done what Harvey did, exactly as he did it. But the difference was that none of them *thought* in the same way that Harvey did. It wasn't that Harvey was necessarily any smarter than they had been, it was simply that he had begun his studies at a time when new ideas of science were coming into their own, and like

An eighteenth-century engraving
of William Harvey with symbols
of his profession: a depiction of
the circulatory system; the opium
poppy, a drug; a staff and a snake,
a variation of the caduceus; and
two medical texts.

Galileo, Kepler, Gilbert, and Bacon, William Harvey had the right kind of mind to grasp the importance of those ideas and use them in his field of work. He was actually one of the world's first real modern scientists, and he made his discovery because he used the methods of modern science—he observed things firsthand, and he conducted experiments to check out the ideas that his observations gave him.

CHAPTER

THE RESULTS
OF HARVEY'S
DISCOVERY

There were still a few unsolved problems in Harvey's explanation of blood circulation, and one of these was how blood got from the arteries to the veins. This was something that couldn't be discovered without a microscope, and Harvey had no microscope.

The microscope was apparently invented by two Dutch eyeglass makers, Johannes Jensen and his son, Zacharias, about 1590, but news of the invention traveled very slowly. Galileo heard of it in 1624 and built a microscope for himself, and soon a number of other scientists were using microscopes for various purposes. But it wasn't until 1661, thirty-three years after the publication of Harvey's book, that an Italian doctor named Marcello Malpighi announced the discovery of capillaries, the tiny vessels connecting arteries to veins, which he had seen with a microscope. This was the last bit of evidence needed to convince everyone that Harvey was completely right.

Now that doctors and medical scientists knew how blood worked, they began to develop ideas they wouldn't have dreamed of before. A young English scientist named Christopher Wren was apparently one of the first to realize that things could be put *into* blood and would then be carried throughout the body. In 1656 he experimented with injecting such substances as wine,

The invention of the microscope in the late sixteenth century opened the way for scientists to see what was not visible to the naked eye. This microscope was made in the seventeenth century by an instrument maker named Marshal.

Vivisection, the use of live animals for scientific research, was common in the seventeenth century. This illustration from a textbook of the time shows the flow of blood through the veins and arteries of a dog.

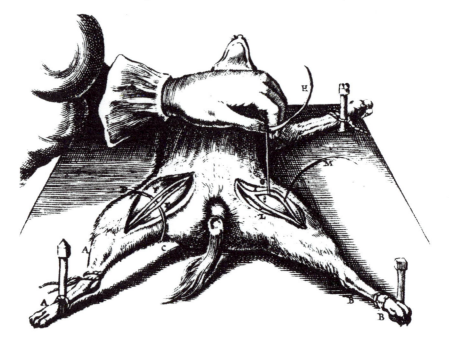

ale, and opium into the bloodstream of a dog to see what the effect would be. Two English doctors followed Wren's experiments with some work of their own. In 1661, Dr. Richard Lower tried to find out if he could keep a dog healthy without feeding it but by injecting beef broth directly into its bloodstream; and in 1663, Dr. Timothy Clarke injected medicines directly into the veins of dogs. Then, in 1666, Dr. Lower piped blood from the vein of one dog directly into the vein of another—the first blood transfusion. Thus, the ideas of intravenous feeding (putting food directly into the bloodstream), injection (putting medicine straight into the bloodstream), and blood transfusion were born as direct results of Harvey's discovery.

When news of Dr. Lower's experiment reached France, a number of French doctors and scientists became interested in blood transfusion. A group known as the Academy Montmort appointed one of its members, Jean Baptiste Denis, to try the experiment, and in March 1667, Denis did a transfusion between two dogs, as Lower had done. But then Denis went further, and in June he performed the first blood transfusion involving a human—twelve ounces of blood from a lamb were piped into the bloodstream of a young man who was suffering from fever and drowsiness. It seems that the young man's condition improved, because it is recorded that his drowsiness left him and that "he grew fatter and was an object of surprise and astonishment to all who knew him."

Despite these successful experiments and new discoveries, doctors still did not understand a number of things that took place during the circulation of blood. For one thing, many doctors and medical scholars still believed that the heart caused some kind of almost magical change in the blood before pumping it out into the body (this idea was left over from the ancient belief in pneuma). For another, it was still a mystery why blood flowing through arteries was bright red while that flowing through veins was dark. This fact had even been used as an argument against Harvey's ideas, with some doctors insisting that the two different colors showed that there were actually two different blood-streams and not just one, as Harvey said.

In 1659 an English doctor named Thomas Willis suggested that when blood went into the heart through the veins a kind of quick, almost magical boiling, or "fermentation," took place, in which the material making up the blood was "loosened," causing it to change color. Many doctors agreed with this, including Richard Lower, who had done the first blood transfusion.

Eight years later Lower and another English scientist, Robert Hooke, began doing experiments to try to find out exactly what happened to blood when it went through the lungs from the right part of the heart to the left. As a result of their work, Lower realized that it was simply the action of the air in the lungs that changed the color of the blood, not anything that happened in the heart itself. In a book he wrote in 1669, Lower said that the change in color from the dark blood of the veins to the bright blood of the arteries was caused by "the penetration of particles of air into the blood." He called these particles "nitrous spirit," meaning a sort of active, life-giving substance. Thus, by means of experiments, Lower had proved what Michael Servetus and Realdo Colombo had really only guessed at a little more than a hundred years earlier—that there was a useful substance in air, which was picked up by blood flowing through the lungs and carried into the body. And by showing that it was this substance that caused the color change in blood rather than some magical activity of the heart, Lower had also proved that the heart did not have any special abilities but was simply a pump, just as Harvey had said.

Although blood transfusion had been shown to be possible, doctors soon discovered it was both difficult and dangerous. Jean Baptiste Denis, who had performed the first transfusion on a human, began doing blood transfusions as treatments for some of his patients, but when one of them died during a transfusion, the French authorities put a stop to any further transfusions in France. In England and elsewhere, experiments with blood trans-

A 1722 engraving of a physician overseeing the blood transfusion from a lamb to a man

fusion soon dwindled away as experimenters found they could not overcome a number of problems, especially the problem of the quick clotting of blood, which made it impossible to use a large amount of blood in a transfusion.

Throughout the eighteenth century, doctors and scientists concentrated mainly on learning about the structure of the heart and the composition, or makeup, of blood. In the late 1700s, Swedish chemist Carl Scheele discovered oxygen, and French chemist Antoine Lavoisier discovered that oxygen is the gas that causes combustion, or burning. Before long doctors were aware that it is oxygen that is picked up by the blood as it goes through the lungs and is carried to all parts of the body, where it is used in the combustion of food to produce the energy that keeps the body alive.

Now that doctors knew that the heart was definitely nothing more than a pump, it wasn't long before some of them began to think about the possibility of replacing a heart with a mechanical pump. In 1812 a French scientist, Julien Legallois, suggested that if blood with oxygen in it could be steadily supplied by a mechanical pump, any part of a body could be kept alive—even a cut-off head! And, in 1828, another Frenchman by the name of Kay showed that Legallois's idea wasn't really too far-fetched, when he kept a detached muscle alive for a period of time by pumping blood into it.

In 1834 an English doctor named James Blundell performed a very important experiment involving blood. Taking blood out of a dog's artery, about an ounce at a time, he put it back into a vein by means of a syringe (the instrument doctors use for giving an injection). He kept this up for about thirty minutes, so that the dog's entire blood supply was taken out and put back in, without the dog suffering any ill effects. What Blundell accomplished with this experiment was to show that circulation of the blood could be extended *outside* the body—blood could be taken out of the body as long as it was quickly put back in at some point farther along its regular path. This was going to be important knowledge for doctors of the future; because of it they were going to be able to hook up a person's circulatory system to mechanical hearts and kidneys outside the body.

Experiments and discoveries continued throughout the 1800s. In 1858, Charles Edouard Brown-Séquard, of France, actually did what Julien Legallois had predicted back in 1812, and kept a dog's head alive for a time by pumping blood into it. In 1866 another Frenchman, Elie de Cyon, removed a frog's heart from its body and kept it alive for forty-eight hours by keeping it steadily supplied with blood. A frog is a cold-blooded, sluggish creature, however, and it was much more difficult to do such a thing with the heart of a warm-blooded, active mammal, such as a dog, cat, or human. It wasn't until 1883 that the problem of keeping a mammal heart alive outside its body was solved by Henry Newell Martin, an American biology professor.

While such experiments may seem pointless and of no value, they were really of tremendous significance, for they were helping to gather the knowledge and information that would eventually enable doctors to operate on diseased hearts. This isn't possible while a heart is beating and blood is passing through it, but once doctors had a way of "disconnecting" a heart and keeping it alive as they worked on it, and of keeping a body alive by means of a mechanical pump to replace the disconnected heart, such an operation was possible. So all these "far-out" experiments of the 1800s were actually stepping-stones toward finding a way of keeping the body and its organs alive by supplying them with blood artificially, and all the experiments were made possible by Harvey's discovery that the heart was a pump.

There were an enormous number of problems to be solved before doctors could even think of doing heart surgery, though. One was the same one that had caused so much trouble to doctors giving transfusions back in the 1600s—the clotting of blood. Blood moving through a tube or pipe outside a body soon clotted and stopped flowing. A number of ways of preventing this had been tried in the 1700s and 1800s, but none were satisfactory. It wasn't until 1916 that a substance was found that could keep blood from clotting without causing possible harm, or even death, to a human being.

As technology improved through the 1900s, more and more new ideas for an artificial heart appeared. Some of these were machines intended to do the work of both the heart and lungs; others were intended only to replace the heart. In 1939 came the first successful use of a machine to take over the work of both heart and lungs, when John H. Gibbon, Jr., an American, kept a cat alive for two hours and fifty-one minutes with blood and oxygen that were circulated through it by means of a special pump. By 1950 there had been similar successful experiments in Sweden, Holland, England, and Belgium, and there were more than thirty different mechanical heart and heart and lung devices.

Harvey's discovery of how the circulatory system works also made another kind of device possible—a machine to do the work of the kidneys. The kidneys are two organs whose main job is to clean body waste products out of the blood as it passes through them. If this can't be done, the body will soon die, so anyone with diseased or damaged kidneys faces certain death. But in 1913 three American doctors invented a way of circulating blood outside the body, through a tube and into a device that cleaned the blood—an artificial kidney—and sent it back into the body through another tube. They tested this device successfully on animals, and twenty-nine years later, in 1942, Dr. Willem Kolff, of Holland, built the first successful artificial kidney system for humans—out of an old washing machine! Today thousands of people are saved from death by having their blood circulate through an artificial kidney, a treatment that is known as *dialysis.*

Nineteen hundred and fifty-one was the year a heart-lung machine was first used for a human. In Minnesota, a six-year-old girl, born with a hole in the septum of her heart, was dying. The only possible way to save her was to try to disconnect her heart and operate to close the hole while keeping her alive with blood

The artificial heart and lung designed by Dr. John H. Gibbon, Jr. The upper tube of the pair being held by the laboratory assistant is attached to a vein, and blood is sucked out by an electric pump which squeezes another rubber tube with a "milking" action. Kept warm in the glass water-bath running diagonally upward in the center of the photograph, the blood flows against the inside lining of the tall steel "lung" cylinder at the left, which rotates several hundred times a minute. The spinning causes the blood to spread in a thin film on the lining, where it absorbs oxygen coming into the cylinder through a tube at the top. The oxygenated blood is then pumped back into the animal.

and oxygen pumped into her by a heart-lung machine. Unfortunately, the little girl died, but the machine performed well enough to make doctors hopeful that similar operations in the future would be successful. And only four months later, Dr. A. Mario Doglietti, of Italy, operated on a man who had a tumor pressing on his heart and used a heart-lung machine to help keep the man alive—the first successful use of such a machine on a human.

Now successes began to come quick and fast. In 1952 the first operation in which a machine completely took over the work of a heart's left side was performed in Detroit. Soon after came an operation in which a machine did the work of a heart's right side. And finally came an operation in which the heart was completely "bypassed" and a machine did all its work.

So, doctors now had one of the things they had been working toward for nearly a century and a half, since Julien Legallois had suggested it in 1812—a machine that could take over the work of a heart, pumping blood and oxygen to all parts of the body to keep them alive. Now, countless lives could be saved—children born with hearts that had holes in them, people whose hearts were injured, and people whose arteries were not working properly. These things could now be corrected by surgery while an artificial heart kept the person alive. But this was not the end of the things that William Harvey had made possible when he discovered that the heart was a pump. Millions of people were dying simply because their hearts were diseased and could no longer do the job of pumping blood through the body. People with such problems couldn't be helped by the kind of machine that was used during heart surgery; what each of them actually needed was a *new* heart to take the place of the diseased one—something that once would have been considered impossible but that doctors and scientists now felt was nearly in their grasp.

There were two ways to accomplish such a thing. One way was to try to make an actual artificial heart, a small mechanical pump that could be put into a human body in place of a real heart.

The other way was to try to replace a diseased heart with the live, healthy heart of another human or perhaps of an animal.

Of course, there were a great many problems with both of these ideas. The main problem in trying to replace a diseased heart with another, healthy heart was that an animal or human part usually just won't work in a body where it doesn't belong—the body simply "rejects" it and it dies. And the problem with an artificial heart was to make it powerful enough—self-powered so that it wouldn't have to have wires leading to an outside battery or generator, completely safe from breaking down (which would kill the person it was in), *and* small enough to fit into a human chest.

Doctors and scientists began working in both directions. In 1957, Dr. Willem Kolff, who had built the first artificial kidney for humans, built a small artificial heart that was connected to an electric pump. He put the heart into a dog and it kept the dog alive for an hour and a half, which proved that an artificial heart could do the work of a living heart. Eleven years later, Dr. Denton Cooley, an American, tried to save a man who was dying of heart disease by implanting an artificial heart in his chest—the first such operation on a human. The artificial heart kept the man alive for more than two days.

Meanwhile, in 1957, Dr. Christiaan Barnard, a South African heading a team of thirty other doctors, performed the first operation to try to replace a diseased human heart with a healthy one. He used the healthy heart of a twenty-five-year-old woman who had been killed in an automobile accident and put it into the body of a fifty-five-year-old man whose own heart was hopelessly damaged. During the operation, the man was kept alive by a heart-lung machine. He lived for eighteen days but then died of a lung infection.

During the 1970s, more transplant operations—replacements of one heart with another—were performed. Most patients died within a year, usually because their bodies finally rejected

Dr. Christiaan Barnard, left, discusses a model of a heart with Dr. Michael de Bakey, center, and Dr. Adrian Kantrowitz, prior to appearing on a TV interview show. Barnard performed the world's first human heart transplant, and de Bakey and Kantrowitz were pioneers in the development of heart aids.

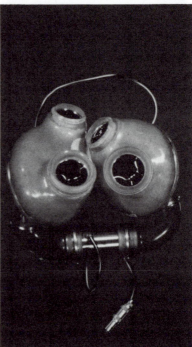

The Jarvik-7 artificial heart. Only slightly larger than a human heart, it has two hollow chambers made of polyurethane. These chambers correspond to the left and right ventricles of the heart.

the new heart. However, by the 1980s this kind of operation was more and more often successful. The biggest problem soon became simply to find enough "replacement" hearts for all the people who needed them.

In 1982, Dr. William De Vries put a new type of artificial heart, invented by Dr. Robert Jarvik, into the chest of a sixty-two-year-old dentist named Barney Clark, who was dying of heart disease. The artificial heart kept Dr. Clark alive for 112 days, working perfectly. But Dr. Clark's illness had gone too far, and things began to go wrong with the rest of his body. He was dying, and rather than keep him alive pointlessly, his doctors turned off the heart.

There have been and there will be other operations to put new hearts or artificial hearts into people who need them. But at this time, there are still problems, especially with the artificial heart. It still must be connected to an outside electric pump and other equipment, which means that a person with an artificial heart cannot walk around or do most of the other things that a person with a real heart can do. Most doctors think that a heart transplant with a real heart offers a better chance for a normal life to someone who has heart disease. They think an artificial heart should only be used to keep a person alive until a real heart can be found. However, some doctors still hope that an artificial heart will eventually be made that has its own power source and won't have to be hooked up to machinery outside its owner's body. They feel that having a supply of such hearts could do away with the major problem of trying to find enough live, healthy hearts for heart transplant operations. But there are a few doctors and scientists who wonder if either artificial hearts *or* transplant operations are really the best answer.

These things will be worked out, one way or another, in the future. But what is really most important is that such things as artificial hearts, heart transplants, dialysis, intravenous feeding, injection of medicine into the bloodstream, and blood transfusions are possible at all. These things have saved millions of lives and will save millions more. They are possible because we now understand completely how the heart and blood work to form the circulatory system. And we understand this because the seventeenth-century English doctor, William Harvey, figured it out, using the methods of modern science.

FURTHER READING

Dunbar, Robert E. *The Heart and Circulatory System*. New York: Franklin Watts, 1984.

Silverstein, Alvin, and Virginia B. *Heartbeats: Your Body, Your Heart*. Philadelphia: Lippincott, 1983.

Ward, Brian. *The Heart and Blood*. New York: Franklin Watts, 1982.

White, Anne Terry, and Gerald S. Lietz. *Secrets of the Heart and Blood*. Easton, Md.: Garrard, 1965.

Zim, Herbert. *Your Heart and How It Works.* New York: Morrow, 1959.

INDEX